T0149686

EDUCATION FROM A MANUFACTURING PERSPECTIVE

A PreK-12 Education Strategy

EDSEL SHEJEN

ARCHWAY PUBLISHING

Archway Publishing books may be ordered through booksellers or by contacting:

Archway Publishing
1663 Liberty Drive
Bloomington, IN 47403
www.archwaypublishing.com
844-669-3957

ISBN: 978-1-6657-0265-2 (sc)
ISBN: 978-1-6657-0266-9 (e)

Library of Congress Control Number: 2021902138

Print information available on the last page.

Archway Publishing rev. date: 02/15/2021

CONTENTS

PREFACE

A close friend of mine received a call one day from her son's school saying that he was having some behavioral issues in class. The principal asked if she would come down to the school and sit in on some of his instruction time to see what was happening and maybe help develop a strategy to bring his behavior under control.

After sitting in one full day of classes my friend noticed that her son was talking to his classmates once his work was complete. When this happened, the teacher demanded he "turn to the front, fold his hands and be quiet until the other students were finished".

At the end of that day the principal called the boy's mother into the office and asked if she saw what was happening and if she had any suggestions about how to improve her son's behavior in class.

My friend responded "yes, give him more work to do." The principal, very surprised, said "We're not talking about his schoolwork; we're talking about his behavior."

She said, "So am I, and you're not keeping him engaged."

The principal became indignant and proclaimed; "We can't do special things for your special child".

To which my friend upped the game a bit more and said; "You're an A—hole. I can do a better job and I don't have millions of dollars in my budget." and that was the beginning of her son's homeschooling.

At around that same time, my nephew had just completed his first year of college and when I went to congratulate him I asked; "Did you feel like high school prepared you for what you faced in your first year?" To which he replied, "Hell no, nothing I took in high school prepared me for *this* year". After hearing his comments I was confused, I knew he took college prep courses in high school and had gotten very good grades. His college grades were good too, but he still had to scramble just to keep up with everyone else.

These two separate but related incidents really made me wonder what was happening in education. I went to public schools and I came away with a very different experience entirely. I loved school. Sure, sports helped keep me on the "straight and narrow", but I understood what school was there for and I felt I was successful.

So, given the above two scenarios, I thought I would take a look at PreK-12 Education from a perspective that I am very familiar with…Manufacturing.

ACKNOWLEDGEMENT

Before I go any further though, I would like to acknowledge the following people that helped make this book and my research possible.

Thank You to:

Laura Webber-Benedetto - for her insights into home schooling, education, technology, engineering and the Arts.

Robert Benedetto - for his insights into education from a teaching and administrative perspective.

David Lowell - for his proof reading skills.

Sara - for her insights into Substance Use Disorder and Mental Health.

Post Script:

As you make your way through the chapters in this book, you may begin to see a pattern.

The chapters begin to setup a step by step process of how to review the business plan of the school district in your community.

Starting with Chapter 2 we begin to look at what may be the roll education plays in the mission of the Declaration of Independence of United States of America.

Chapter 3 lays out the general business structure of the School Committee and Superintendant relationship.

In Chapter 4 we start to look at minimum requirements for effective learning in a classroom.

Chapter 5 shows a general outline for an effective educational system from the perspective of a manufacturing one.

Chapter 6 provides an outline for a typical Career Development Process to be in place for high school students to be college and career ready.

Next is Chapter 7, and it provides a Summary Outline of the core systems that need to be fully in place and functional before the entire machine can work. This outline ties all the working parts together and creates a way to step back and take an overall look at the system itself.

You may want to use Chapter 8 as an example of how to track your district for required action items as identified in the previous chapter.

Finally Chapter 9 includes documents that contain topics you will refer to for monitoring or auditing the school district in your community.

When all the chapters are combined, we have an effective auditing tool that will help identify problems in any education system.

INTRODUCTION

My name is Edsel Shejen, I grew up in York, Maine and went to York schools. After graduating, I attended a local trade school for Machine Tool Processes and spent thirty six years in manufacturing.

During that time, there were four metrics that were drilled into our heads - Safety, Quality, Schedule and Cost. We would say that we wanted to "safely, produce a quality product, on time at the lowest cost".

After these metrics were established, the departments within the shop used established problem solving systems such as Lean Manufacturing, Deming Principles, Quality Circles etc. to identify problems, determine causes and implement solutions that gave the greatest impact for the least cost. We monitored metrics after solution implementation to determine the effectiveness of our recommendations.

After I retired from manufacturing I decided to take the problem solving skills that I had learned and apply them to education.

I organized these skills into the form of an audit and conducted that audit on the school district in my area.

The audit included -

1. A review of the district and school websites
2. Interviews with former students and parents.
3. Attending six months worth of school committee meetings and review of meeting minutes.
4. View of federal and state assessments of the schools in the district.

These were my recommended actions:

I. Develop a Team Oriented District Mission (Careers, Civic Duty, Life to the Fullest) - Develop a mission oriented culture, with continuity, and put in place administrators, leaders and teachers with the training, instructions, tools and materials to safely, provide a quality education, on time, at the lowest cost for every student.

II. Create a Strategic Plan with Continuous Improvement Principles to carry out that mission - Adopt a proven, superior, written, transparent, education plan, aligned with the district's mission, is based on continuous improvement principles, is accepted locally as well as nationwide and includes the option to modify or drop it when not living up to expectations.

III. Communicate to the Public using an Education Dashboard - Display for review by the community in an education dashboard "real time" metrics that measure successes and are a definition of the district's mission.

IV. Incorporate Staff Development Strategies - A review by the district to determine the involvement, relationship and effectiveness of performance evaluations, professional development, position descriptions and personnel recruitment strategies as they relate to this system.

V. Implement Effective Corporate Level Differentiated Instruction Programs or "Individual Tutoring in a Classroom Environment" and include all learning styles and needs - Implement at a corporate level intuitive teaching programs that are based on "individual tutoring in a classroom environment" where students can progress independently and at peak levels.

VI. Develop Proactive Intervention Strategies (Basic Needs, Behavior and Academic Guidance):

a. Community Support Programs - Determining the extent of involvement in community support programs is a great way to start to determine the numbers of students committed to the mission, but after these basic numbers are established we need to go deeper. Prioritization of the remaining individual students at risk, will give a better idea of the work involved in completing the mission.

b. "Teach/Learn" mode vs. "Infraction/Penalty" mode - Don't institute a penalty to avoid a learning moment. Wide sweeping policies that group students together to apply a single remedy for what may be a very individual and personal situation, only aggravates an already difficult situation. There are no shortcuts to keeping students on track. Every student requires connectivity to achieve peak performance.

c. Academic Intervention Strategies - Using continuous improvement principles, utilize a tiered approach in dealing with struggling performance. Support systems, skill enhancement and specialized instruction may be needed, while not forgetting connectedness.

d. Required Connectivity - Initiating interventions for wellbeing, behavior, special needs, motivation etc. and insuring engagement through Steam, extra-curricular activities, nature based programs, entrepreneurship etc. is a more direct approach in helping students connect to the best path.

e. Career Development (professional, kinetic or both) – This is the minimum required message to students going forward: "As a member of this community, you're part of a family. As a family we are on a mission to prepare you to be independent, a contributor to your community and live your life to the fullest. Your contribution is so valuable we cannot risk it. Let's work together, as a team, to prepare you for the task ahead by supporting your individuality, clearing a path for you to excel and connect you to it."

f. Continuous Determination of Need – We will conduct a thorough search, using continuous improvement principles, for any potential student in our area of responsibility that has a need for assistance.

EDUCATION PHILOSOPHY

If, "We the People", believe that the United States of America is an experiment in self governance then there are a few basic truths that we need to acknowledge.

When the founding fathers set the ground work for this system of government, their visions were loftier than even they could have envisioned.

Beginning with the Declaration of Independence, the first sentences proclaim that "all men (humankind) are created equal" and that they are "endowed by their creator with certain unalienable rights, that among these are life, liberty and the pursuit of happiness".

From this, the United States Constitution was drafted to layout the guidelines for a system of government that fulfills the mission of that declaration.

Established within this system were three "separate but equal" branches of government:

The legislative branch, elected "by the people", enacts laws and oversees actions by the executive branch.

The judicial branch, with judges appointed by the president and approved by the Senate, makes decisions on the constitutionality of legislative actions.

The executive branch, also elected "by the people", carries out the actions of the legislative branch and protects the nation through executive orders.

Within the executive branch are departments that make up the president's cabinet who carry out the mission as outlined in legislation and guided by the constitution.

These departments are separated by basic mission functions;

1. National Security (influence by outside forces) Department of State, Department of Defense, Department of Homeland Security, National Intelligence Agency – These departments protect the United States of America from foreign actors that wish to undermine.
2. Interior (environmental protection) Department of the Interior, Environmental Protection Agency – These departments preserves our environment.
3. Currency (monetary exchange and taxation) Department of Treasury – Maintains a system of fair monetary exchange and taxation.
4. Infrastructure (facilities) Department of Transportation, Department of Energy – Maintains a system of transport and sustainability.

5. Trade (Goods Manufactured and Exchanged) Department of Commerce, Small Business Administration – A fair system of national and international commerce.
6. "The People" (equality, life, liberty and the pursuit of happiness) Department of Health and Human Services, Department of Agriculture, Department of Housing and Urban Development, Department of Education, Department of Labor, Department of Veterans Affairs – How the mission is defined.
7. Justice (equal opportunity under the law) Department of Justice – When the system fails and people fall through the cracks, we as a people, have not completed the mission.

Once we begin to establish security, environmental protection, monetary stability and an infrastructure that supports trade (The cake that everyone cuts from) we can focus in on the true mission defined by the Declaration of Independence.

If we see this mission as assuring that "all men (humankind) are created equal" and that they are "endowed by their creator with certain unalienable rights, that among these are life, liberty and the pursuit of happiness" then this is our metric to measure success.

If we believe that people remanded to the justice system is a metric to show government's ineffectiveness then that system of justice becomes only a form of internal security, not a tool for completing the mission.

Providing citizens with the potential to earn enough to live, give back to society and live life with liberty and to the fullest are where we need to focus. That means focusing on "The People" as a unit right down to the state and local level monitored by the "free press".

If we believe our children's education is a big step toward completion of the mission, then this makes children are our most precious resource. If children are never to blame and no child wants to fail then we as adults are accountable.

I understand that some teachers do not want to be held accountable for student performance. I understand that administrators do not want to tell teachers how to teach and I even understand elected officials not wanting to have metrics hanging over their heads that show education performance in their district. The problem is; this is about learning.

SCHOOL COMMITTEE AND SUPERINTENDANT

BUSINESS PHILOSOPHY

Generally, when business is faced with an issue, the action taken is directed at only that issue.

All actions taken, due to these issues, must be viewed from an overall strategy and show a change to the bottom line (Safety, Quality, Schedule, Cost); otherwise the investment is just another exercise in spending money.

To verify the action taken has had an effect on the bottom line, clear quantifiable data that shows performance, before and after the action, must be evaluated to determine the actual benefit.

For as long as the business strategy is to manage crisis and disregard the need to take an operational viewpoint instead of one of crisis, resolution to any problems will never be realized.

What is the goal?

- Improvement in Safety, Quality, Schedule, Cost.

How do we define the goal?

- Recurring Quantified Data
- Charts – with defined key performance data

Is the path to the goal defined?

- Documented Organizational Structure, Standards and Strategy for Manpower, Training, Instructions, Tools and Materials.

Are obstacles to the goal defined?

- Determine parts of the Organizational Structure, Standards and Strategy that are impeding performance.

Determine actions to eliminate obstacles.

- Clearly defined with milestones.

How do we ensure actions taken are maintained?

- Regular Attention (continuous improvement principles) - audits, two-way communications with employees
- Enforcement – disciplinary action.

HIERARCHY

1. Creation of an Operations Manger;
2. Regular Operational Meetings (day, time, cycle) with employee department heads for management of systems outlined below. All actions will be documented in standards and posted on Website.
   a. By-Laws, Mission Statement, Vision, Slogan, Strategy, Operational Standards, Project Database with Responsible Official, Project Elevation Requirements and Milestones. Include two-way communications with employees on actions/ effects.
   b. Published performance metrics (Safety, Quality, Schedule, Cost).
   c. Operational Dashboard (Standards, Department Hierarchy, Strategy) to reflect changes to Manpower, Training, Work Instructions, Tools, Materials.
   d. Service Level Agreements with service providers.
   e. Work Skills Updates –
      1) Lesson Plans for safety/skills
      2) On The Job Training - Skill signoff by department heads
      3) Training in following and developing Lesson Plans
      4) Connect deficiencies to required skills.
   f. Asset Management – Maintenance, Utilization, Capacity, Capability, Continuity, Procurement, Justification, Requirements, Database.
   g. Training Plans for Repetitive Work – Required "step by step" plan to complete requirements based on previous "trial and error" that is efficient and cost effective.

h. Outside Review of Operations -
1) Initiate survey of business operations for review, make needed changes and reflect in items a-g.
2) Setup follow-up reviews periodically.

BUSINESS PLAN PERIODIC REVIEW

Managers are to ask the following questions and view operations from an overall business strategy.

1. Regular Operational Meetings – What do the staff meetings look like and how often do you meet?
2. Business Structure – What is the current structure (standards), what format is it in and how visible to the employees is it?
3. Performance Metrics – What are the metrics (Safety, Quality, Schedule, Cost) and how visible are they?
4. Service Level Agreements – Who are the service providers and what standards are they required to meet?
5. Work Skills – What training programs are in place, do they address the skills required for the business, are the training plans detailed and how do they address the metrics?
6. Asset Management – What asset management processes are in place, what are the assets capabilities, capacities, utilization, justification, procurement processes/ requirements?
7. Training Plans – What are the documented methods for performing work in the business?
8. Objective Business Review – When was the last objective outside review of operations?

TEACHING

INTRODUCTION

I've been studying teaching methods since teaching students martial arts in 1973. I have developed this plan from my own experiences along with those of some of the best athletes in the world in a wide variety of sports.

Not everyone is going to bench press five hundred pounds, run the forty yard dash in four seconds or dance like Michael Jackson. On the other hand, with the proper instruction, everyone should be able to correctly perform the bench press, run the forty yard dash and do the "Moon Walk".

A former colleague of mine was an instructor for the machinist apprenticeship at the Portsmouth Naval Shipyard in Kittery, Me. He would always say, "Give me someone with the basic abilities and desire and I'll make them a good machinist".

"There are no bad students, only bad teachers", Ryron Gracie Brazilian Jujitsu Master.

ASSIMILATION

Before we setup a teaching strategy, let's look at the ways that students' best learn.

There are five basic ways that information gets assimilated and each student uses different combinations of these learning styles due to individual differences. The teacher must pay close attention to each student during the teaching process to determine the students' best combination of learning styles.

The learning styles are:

1. Visual – blackboard, presentations, demonstrations, video etc.
2. Audio – various sounds and the spoken word.
3. Kinetic – hands on training or learn by doing.
4. Progressive – begin with basic concepts then to more complex.
5. Spatial – seeing the finish product and mentally breaking down the parts.

The first four are fairly common knowledge to most instructors but "Spatial" is a method that is commonly overlooked. Spatial learning helps the student see where the course material will take them and its' place in the big picture.

STRATEGY

For the learning experience to be successful requires a few things:

1. The student (and guardian if applicable) must come to class with;
   a. The basic psychological and physiological capabilities to learn.

   This is determined through a collaborative effort with the student (and guardians if needed), health care professionals, teachers and family members.

   Whenever a student has learning difficulties the first root causes to be investigated are usually the more common clinically defined ones. While these should not be ruled out, we also should look at more common difficulties as well. Performance difficulties can often be linked to substance use disorder, medications, hunger, sleep deprivation, course load, work, family and social life. All these roads must be cleared before learning can resume.
   b. The desire to do the same.

   In all my years coaching, teaching and competing I have never met anyone who wanted to fail. The desire to succeed is a given.

   The above being said, there is a distinct correlation between need and desire. The student may have the "need" to accomplish a lesser goal that is on the way to a larger one but does not show the "desire" to attain the lesser goal. It is often up to the teacher to transfer that need to desire.
2. The instructor must include the following in the teaching program –
   a. Assessment – Prior to instruction, an overall assessment of the student's abilities should be accomplished to correctly place the student in the program.

   Periodically, during instruction, the teacher must determine if the student is progressing as desired based on material to be covered and the time allotted. These assessments are conducted throughout the learning process and observations of shortfalls should create "recommendations" for timely progress toward the student's goals. All assessments include two-way communication and should be done with a positive tone. Negativity only clouds the view to the end goal. Believe the student will reach their goals with your help.

   Placement within the program depends on initial and subsequent assessments and goals to be attained. Performance at the highest level is always the goal. Program Levels:

Level 1 – Basic technical performance
Level 2 – Functional proficiency
Level 3 – Artistic interpretation

The grade achieved within the current program level is based on the understanding, performance and recognition of the practical applications of the material within that level.
Grading Scale:

Grade 1 – Continue working
Grade 2 – Meets basic requirements
Grade 3 – Advance

Program Levels and Grading Scale are for efficiency of instruction only and should not be used to notify the student of their progress. Student notification of performance level could stifle potential.

b. Logical Progression – Information is presented in a logical systematic order from most basic to more difficult with the most basic being building blocks to the more complex.
c. Association – seeing the work being done and being able to emulate that work helps to bring the curriculum to practice.
d. Artistic Interpretation – when students perform the work and give it their' own "personal touch", the material is solidified and becomes a personal interpretation. (There will only ever be one Michael Jackson "Moon Walk").

A teaching plan that safely produces the required effect 100 percent of the time, in a timely manner and at the lowest cost is the goal. Any adjustments must have an effect on this bottom line (Safety-Quality-Schedule-Cost).

TEACHER EVALUATION AND PROGRAM MINIMUM REQUIREMENTS

1. Student Capability Assessments
   a. All support cast included
   b. Psychological and Physiological difficulties
      1/ Clinical
      2/ Common
      3/ General Student Enthusiasm (positive, negative, indifferent or just bored)

2. Teaching Program
    a. Assessments - initial and periodic
        1/ Time Spans - Multiple
        2/ Documentation of Student progress
        3/ Personal Communication Skills
        4/ Teacher Positive Attitude
        5/ Success of Recommendations
        6/ Tiered Placement within Program
            a- Level 1-
            b- Level 2-
            c- Level 3-
        7/ Grading Style
            a- Learning-
            b- Performing-
            c- Advance-
    b. Visual Instruction
        1/ Overheads, Blackboard and Video
    c. Audio Instruction
        1/ Lectures, Recordings
    d. Logical Progression
        1/ Documented, Logical Order
        2/ Basic building blocks to the more complex
    e. Kinetic (Hands On)
        1/ Student learns by actually performing the work
    f. Spatial
        1/ Able to see the finished product and break down the parts
3. Adaptation of Student Learning Styles in Lesson Plans
    a. Note coverage of learning styles for students in classroom through documented student interviews.
4. Teacher Performance Metrics
    a. Safety –
    b. Quality –
    c. Schedule –
    d. Cost –

GENERAL STRUCTURE (CHECKLIST)

a. Goals
   1) Goal Statements - definitive, quantitative and to the point
      a- Preparing 100 percent of students for careers, civic life and self enrichment.
         1- Define Metrics
   2) Subjects required – core, expressive, team building, project development., etc.
   3) Education grading system - requirements, timeline and milestones
      a- Local/State/Federal assistance – funding, technical support, legal action
b. Strategy
   1) Progression
      a- Elementary – Basic skills with broad foundation
      b- Middle – Preparation for self-direction in High School
      c- High - Programs for career, civic life and self-enrichment
   2) Strategy of a Strategy
      a- Adopt a proven, superior, written, transparent, education plan, aligned with the district's mission, is based on continuous improvement principles, includes every child, is accepted locally as well as nationwide and includes the option to modify or drop it when not living up to expectations.
c. Visibility
   1) Education Dashboard
      a- Metrics – Definition of the Mission
         1- Safety
            a/ Maintain minimum required attendance of students/staff
         2- Quality
            a/ Metrics to prepare 100 percent of students for careers, civic life and self enrichment
            b/ Teacher/Principal Evaluation and Professional Growth
         3- Schedule
            a/ Teach to child development level
         4- Cost
            a/ Classroom size is the result of completing education goals

                b/ Required funding, tech support and legal action to complete goals

          b- Standards

              1- Policies and procedures for manpower, training, instructions, tools and materials needed to complete goals.

          c- Structure

              1- School and District Departments and POCs

          d- Strategy

              1- Prepare students for careers, civic life and self-enrichment

d. Teacher Quality

    1) Performance Evaluations

        a- Student Capability Assessments

            1- Total Cast

            2- Difficulties

                a/ Clinical

                b/ Common

                c/ General Attitude

        b- Teaching Program

            1- Periodic Assessments – Over the Shoulder, time spans

            2- Learning Styles – Visual, Audio, Progressive, Kinetic, Spatial

            3- Peak Performance - Individual instruction in a classroom environment, proficiency as a minimum requirement

        c- Behavioral, Guidance, Academic collaboration while grading separately. Maintain an environment conducive to learning.

        d- Collaborate with teachers of related and prerequisite subjects.

        e- Documented Parent and Student Interviews

        f- Metrics (Safety, Quality, Schedule, Cost)

    2) Trade Skill Development

        a- Teacher development programs based on school requirements

        b- Link school metrics and teacher performance appraisals to local work skill lesson plans.

e. Principal Quality

    1) Performance Evaluations

        a- Student Capability Assessments

            1- Total Cast

            2- Difficulties

                a/ Clinical

                b/ Common

                c/ General Attitude

      b- School Continuous Improvement Learning Program

          1- Periodic Assessments – major points, observe, converse, document

          2- Career Preparation Process – kinetic, degree or both

          3- Peak Performance – Individual Tutoring in a Classroom Environment; course load based on child development level and proficiency as a minimum requirement.

      c- Behavioral, Guidance, Academic collaboration while grading separately. Maintain an environment conducive to learning

      d- Teachers collaborate in related subjects

      e- Documented Parent and Student Interviews

      f- Metrics (Safety, Quality, Schedule, Cost)

    2) Trade Skill Development

      a- Principal development programs based on district requirements.

      b- Link school metrics and performance appraisals to local work skill lesson plans.

f. Maintaining Quality Staff

    1) Create Position Descriptions -

      a- Maintain structure

    2) Create Evaluations -

      a- Maintain structure

      b- Maintain historical assessment results

    3) Provide Training (Contractor, On Job Training, Work Skill Training)

      a- Maintain structure

      b- Maintain historical assessment results

g. Corporate Automated Differentiated Instruction Programs, (CADIP) "Individual Tutoring in a Classroom Environment" (KAHN, IXL)

a. Includes all learning styles and needs

h. Address metric deficiencies

    1) Safety -

      a- Review of Manpower, Training, Instructions, Tools and Materials in Position Descriptions/Evaluations/Training

    2) Quality –

      a- Same as above with review of Safety issues as well.

    3) Schedule –

      a- Same as above with review of Safety and Quality issues as well.

    4) Cost –

      a- Review Safety, Quality and Schedule issues. (Cost is the result of completing the first three goals).

i. Parent/Community Involvement
   1) Parent/Community review of local educational systems
      a- Website School – Dashboard, Parent Login, Contacts
      b- Website District – Dashboard, Contacts
      c- Website State – Report Card, Legislation, Support
      d- Website United States – Legislation, State Status
   2) Parental Support
      a- Attendance
      b- Homework
      c- Activities
      d- Parent-Teacher Conferences
j. Social Work Guidelines
   1. Counseling
   2. History
   3. Adaptability
   4. Commitment
   5. Hope
   6. Connectedness
   7. Trust
   8. Leadership
   9. Community
   10. Persevere
   11. Spirituality
   12. Stability

CAREER PREPARATION PROCESS

I. Create Electronic Resume (or subscribe to commercial website)
1. General student Info (email, address, phone, school, coaches, Parents-Guardians, Self Essay)
2. Academic info such as GPA, Transcripts, SAT, ACT, Subject Tests
3. Develop Highlight Videos and Pictures (see section on Highlight Videos).
4. List awards, Interests, Stats, Goals
5. Document other related/non-related activity stats, dates, times, coach/POC info etc.
6. If subscribing to websites, be sure they provide instructional videos, seminars, webinars, conference calls, articles, emails and POC's to help through recruiting process and to navigate their website.

II. School/Coach Contact Strategies
1. Use college search engines or electronic maps to develop a list of up to 200 schools with required major, sports/activities of interest, coach/POC contact information, other areas of interest and desired geographic area.
2. Pick about 20 schools from the above list to watch carefully for your "wish list". Include any schools that you may have an inside track to. If good grades, watch Ivy's – they love STUDENT athletes/participants.
3. Develop standard phone messages and emails with athlete/participant contact info for coaches/POCs of schools of interest:
   a- Dear Coach/Prof/Advisor _____ I am very interested in playing/participating in/for your team/program, it has been a dream of mine to play/participate at the next level for a long time.
   b- I am from _____ and I play/participate for _____
   c- Brief history of your stats and where info can be viewed
   d- I'll be calling you again at _____ on _____
   e- End with athlete/participant contact info – Name, address, email, cell, regular phone, fax etc.

4. Create from information in the section above a printable, one page, well styled scout report to be mailed, emailed and handed to coaches/officials (see section on One Page Scouting Report).

5. Conduct mass mail distributions including scouting report to all coaches and POC's.

III. Narrow school selections

1. Develop spread sheet with 1-10 point rating system based on desired academics, athletics/activity, geographic location, scholarships, cost and other benefits for ranking schools.

2. Document history of coach/POC communications (Emails, Letters, Calls, Camps and visits etc.) and use this information to weigh offers as well.

3. After responses to distribution letters, re-calculate top 10 schools based on point rating system, offers or any other in-side track you might have. Be sure to evaluate scholarship types and limits (actual awards, considerations, evaluations, referrals, injuries, making the team etc.). Direct pursue contacts with any schools that you are still keen on to get one more chance at them before they are cut from the list.

4. Pick at least your top three to five to visit(you may visit more depending affordability or if the school is paying for an official visit).

5. You are ready to put in applications!

IV. Timeline Senior Year

1. September – Organize
    a. Determine Top Schools
    b. Determine Application Deadlines
    c. Clean up shortfalls on requirements – SAT, ACT, Classes
    d. Contact guidance counselor to start process as they are familiar with many schools, applications, essays, contacts, tendencies, Letter/s of Recommendation, Common Applications.
    e. Letters of Recommendation (if required) – pick and notify POC and include deadline.
    f. Determine early action schools.

2. October – Early Action Application
    a. Fill out early action applications (early decision if this is your school of choice)

3. November – Letters, Essays
    a. Write Essay
    b. Check progress on Letter/s of Recommendation.
    c. Gain access to FAFSA, Common App and links to tests and transcripts for college applications.

4. December – Applications
   a. Begin applications and load FAFSA with financial info.
   b. Late business – new Visits, Applications, Offers, Correspondence.
5. January – FAFSA update
   a. FAFSA update and submit with College codes.
   b. Apply for outside Scholarships (See Appendix C: Websites and Organizations").

V. Financial Aid Senior Year
   1. Filling out FAFSA – fill out paper form of this first with previous year's financial data. This makes the first of the year easier and on January 1, just update information and send. Financial aid is on first come first serve basis, so file as close to Jan 1 as possible.
   2. Financial Aid terms:
      COA (Cost Of Attending) - this is what financial aid is based on, all costs to attend.
      EFC (Expected Family Contribution) - what the government says your family can afford to contribute.
      NEED – the difference between COA and EFC
   3. Find schools that cover as close to 100 percent need as possible.
   4. Determine breakdown of need.
      a. Scholarships/Grants – money given to you that you do not pay back
      b. Loans – money that gets paid back in payments with interest after graduation. These can be many types, fixed rate, govt., variable, private etc.
      c. Work Study - A job that is given to the student to earn a percentage of COA. Try to get a job that does not interfere with the season of your sport.
   5. Leverage – competition of school programs (engineering, science, art), Athletic divisions (1A, 1AA, II, III), conferences (NESCAC, NE-10, BIG 10).
   6. Appeals Letter – to leverage similar offers for best possible price.
      a. NCSA/Guidance provide copy.
      b. Include a copy of competing offer.

VI. Admission Strategy – Notes
   1. This approach will work for all students of all back grounds with a variety interests. Students are a commodity for schools, involvement in sports, arts, activities and sciences etc. enhance the college experience and increase the school's value.
   2. Visit as many schools as possible, as early as possible.
   3. Keep coaches/administrators involved throughout process to reduce fees and eliminate road blocks. Include them in emails, notify of competing offers and use them to get current status of admission progress.

4. Be sure to ask if schools stack funding. Coaches/Administrators may find additional sources of funding but if one type of funding just replaces another, it does not help the bottom line.

5. Ask current students about their school, activities, financial aid and if their funding has been consistent throughout their career.

6. Aim high but have a good cushion – have safe schools or alternate routes to your career goals in case top choices fall through.

7. Above all - ASK QUESTIONS!

VII. High School Guidance Questions (Y/N fill-in)

1. ____ Career goals and academic program determined as soon as possible (College, Vocation, Apprenticeship, Entry Level Work Program etc.) beginning of sophomore year at a minimum? This decision is made with Guidance Counselor, Parents and Student involvement.

2. ____ Does your school have an electronic or manual method to send updated versions of transcripts, test scores etc. for inclusion with college applications? Receipt of these items by the college verified by the student through this program?

3. ____ CommonApp.com – guidance through the process (Not with a local vendor or college)? Many schools use the same application form, fill it out once!

4. ____ FAFSA – guidance through the process (Not with a local vendor or college)? Definition of terms below.
   1) Grants – Need, Special Circumstances, Minorities.
   2) Scholarships – Academic, Merit, Activities.
   3) Loans – Types
   4) Work Study – Types

5. ____ SAT/ACT Strategy
   1) PSAT Sophomore – analysis of weaknesses and strategy to correct. This is preparation for competition not a test of qualification.
   2) SAT Prep Courses – time management, subject strengths and weaknesses, skipping, section strategies etc.
   3) Number of attempts and gains vs. cost.
   4) Availability of additional Subject Tests required by colleges.

6. ____ College Essay courses (Parent Review)

7. ____ Reference requirements with student verification of completion (Parent Review)

8. ____ Treat this process like a job search
   1) Section I Sophomore – Resume
   2) Section II Junior – Distribution
   3) Section III Senior – Process to narrow offers (See Section IV Timeline)

9. ___ Students and Parents informed of the gravity of this decision, this could create debt that they will be paying for many years ($250K for 20-30yrs @ up to $200 – $500/mo).

APPENDIX A: WEBSITES AND ORGANIZATIONS

1. Athletics:
   Scout.com
   Maxpreps.com
   Rivals/highscool.com
   National Underclassmen Combine
   NCSA
2. College search engines and databases:
   Petersons.com
   http://nces.ed.gov/collegenavigator
   Federalstudentaid.ed.gov/choosing
   http://www.noodle.org/colleges
3. College Scholarship and grant opportunities:
   Groups – Kiwanis, Lions, Eagles, Elks, Rotary, American Legion etc.
   Businesses - Parents Employers
   Colleges - School Alumni and Admissions Representative
   Special Conditions relating to major
   Reciprocity – special considerations for out of state students
   Websites –
   > Scholarships.com
   > Collegeanswer.com
   > Collegetoolkit.com
   > Collegenet.com/mach25
   > Mesfoundation.com
   > Collegeview.com
   > Schoolsoup.com
   > Studentaid.com
   > Finaid.org
   > Studentaid.ed.gov
   > Students.gov
   > Financial Aid Application - www.FAFSA.com
4. CSS Financial Aid Profile – https://profileonline.collegeboard.com

5. College Common Application – www.commonapp.com
6. Calculator School Cost – https://netprocecalculator.collegeboard.org
7. FAFSA Forecaster – www.fafsa4caster.ed.gov
8. High School web links for upload of transcripts, references, self-essays and tests etc.

SUMMARY OUTLINE

I. Team Oriented Mission – Careers, Civic Duty, Life to the Fullest.
    a. Determine goals as a metric definition of the mission
    b. Include requirements, timeline and milestones for funding, technical support and legal action
II. Strategic Plan
    a. Status of action items
III. Dashboard – Strategic Plan, Standards, Structure, Metrics
    a. Management of capacity, capability, continuity, Cpk
IV. Evaluations, Professional Growth, Job Descriptions, Recruitment
    a. Manpower, Training, Instructions, Tools, Materials
V. Effective Corporate Automated Differentiated Instruction Programs (CADIPs), "Individual Tutoring in a Classroom Environment" (KAHN Academy, IXL)
    a. Includes all learning styles and needs
VI. Proactive Intervention Strategy – Welfare, Behavior, Guidance, Academics.
    a. Community Support Programs
    b. "Teach/Learn" mode vs. "Infraction/Penalty" mode
    c. Academic Intervention Strategies
        1) Tier1 (Whole Child), Tier2 (Skills), Tier3 (Special Needs)
    d. Required Connectivity
        1) Academics, Art, Tech, Athletics, Science, Entrepreneurial, Service etc.
    e. Career Development – Professional, Kinetic or both
        1) Regional Tech Centers, Common App, Naviance
    f. Continuous Determination of Need

I.   Develop a Team Oriented District Mission (Careers, Civic Duty, Life to the Fullest)

     a.   Determine goals as a metric definition of the mission. Include requirements, timeline and milestones with funding, technical support and legal action.

         Summary: Develop a mission oriented culture, with continuity, and put in place administrators, leaders and teachers with the training, instructions, tools and materials to safely, provide a quality education, on time, at the lowest cost for every student.

II. Creation of a Strategic Plan with Continuous Improvement Principles

     a.   Develop a communication tool with the public for status of action items.

         Summary: Adopt a proven, superior, written, transparent, education plan, aligned with the district's mission, is based on continuous improvement principles, is accepted locally as well as nationwide and includes the option to modify or drop it when not living up to expectations.

III. Communication to the Public using an Education Dashboard

     a.   Safety, Quality, Schedule, Cost

         Summary: Display for review by the community in an Education Dashboard "real time" metrics that measure successes and are a definition of the district's mission.

IV. Staff Development Strategies - Performance Evaluations, Professional Development, Position Descriptions, Personnel Recruitment Strategies within a Continuous Improvement System.

     a.   Manpower, Training, Instructions, Tools, Materials

         Summary: A review by the district to determine the involvement, relationship and effectiveness of evaluations, development, position descriptions and recruitment strategies as they relate to this system.

V.   Effective Corporate Automated Differentiated Instruction Programs, "Individual Tutoring in a Classroom Environment" (KAHN Academy, IXL)

     a.   Includes all learning styles and needs

         Summary: Implement at a corporate level Intuitive teaching programs that are based on "individual tutoring in a classroom environment" where students can progress independently and at peak levels.

VI. Proactive Intervention Strategy – Welfare, Behavior, Guidance, Academics

     a.   Community Support Programs

         Summary: Determining the extent of involvement in community support programs is a great way to start to determine the numbers of kids committed to "careers, civic responsibility and self-enrichment", but after the numbers are established we need to go deeper. Prioritization of the remaining individual students at risk, through proven intervention programs (internally data driven), will give a better idea of the work involved in conquering these issues.

b. "Teach/Learn" mode vs. "Infraction/Penalty" mode

Summary: Don't institute a penalty to avoid a learning moment. Wide sweeping policies that group students together to apply a single remedy for what may be a very individual and personal situation, only aggravates an already difficult situation. There are no shortcuts to keeping students on track. Every student requires connectivity to achieve peak performance.

c. Academic Intervention Strategies

Summary: Using continuous improvement principles, utilize a tiered approach in dealing with struggling performance. Support systems, skill enhancement and specialized instruction may be needed not forgetting "required connectivity".

d. Required Connectivity

Summary: Initiating interventions (Wellbeing, Behavior, Special Needs, Motivation etc.) and insuring engagement through STEAM, extra-curricular activities, nature based programs, entrepreneurship, service etc. is a more direct approach in helping students connect to the best path.

e. Career Development – professional, kinetic or both

Summary: The message: "As a member of this school community, you're part of a family. As a family we are on a mission to prepare you to be independent, a contributor to society and to live your life to the fullest. Your contribution is so valuable we cannot risk it. Let's work together, as a team, to prepare you for the task ahead by supporting your individuality, clearing a path for you to excel and connect you to it."

f. Continuous Determination of Need.

Summary: Conduct a thorough search, using continuous improvement principles, for students that have a need for assistance.

AUDIT ACTION ITEMS

I.   Mission - Maintain, with student buy-in, a Team Oriented Mission Culture
     Inspiration (Messages - walls, teacher/admin spaces, discussions), Motivation (successes),
Connectedness (participation), Acceptance (individuality), Direction (path), Collaboration
(culture), Continuity(efficiency), Capability(areas), Capacity(volume), CpK (effectiveness)
     Foster a mission culture of inspiration through core messages, motivation by review
of past successes, connectivity through activity participation, acceptance by encouraging
student individuality, direction by connecting students to the best path, and collaboration
by bringing people together through a common cause all perpetuated by interactions with
staff, students and support systems with successes measured through low levels of bullying
and high levels of ex/co-curricular activity participation.

> Supporting Metrics – Climate (Education Dashboard)
> Bullying (Number of reports filed, open)
> Co/Ex Curricular Activity Participation (percent Involvement/school)
> Published to PII requirements

II. Instruction - Corporate Automated Differentiated Instruction Programs (CADIPs)
     Continuity (efficiency), Capability (areas), Capacity (volume), CpK (effectiveness)
     Include instruction that develops continuity, capability and capacity in all subjects
and grade levels by utilizing Corporate Automated Differentiated Instruction Programs
(CADIPs) with their effectiveness measured through average performance ratings and
proficiency levels.

> Supporting Metrics – Instruction (Education Dashboard)
> Performance Evaluations (Average Yearly Progress)
> CADIPs (Average Yearly Progress)
> Published to PII requirements

JUSTIFICATION

Mission - Maintain, with student buy-in, a Team Oriented Mission Culture

Recently I attended open houses in all schools. This is what I observed:

1. Outstanding Individual Teacher Contributions – As I walked from classroom to classroom, in all four facilities, I noticed fantastic student achievements posted on walls inside classrooms. Every teacher was beaming with pride over the programs they headed and what their students had accomplished.

2. Parent/Staff Introductions - At the high school and middle school I attended introductions to staff for parents and guardians.

    They were informative, well organized and most of all, seemed to put the newly admitted parent's minds at ease. Schools had handouts with maps and directions to classrooms, guides for parents to use in assisting their children with homework and information on how to get involved in their school's activities.

3. Sub Contractors – Another observation that I made was the number of sub-contractors that the school system uses or endorses.

    The use of contractors to help with "production overflow" has long been accepted by manufacturing but not for implementation of the mission. Core mission beliefs are carried out by the organization or it has very finely tuned RFQs that clearly identify goals, metrics and evaluation methods all inside a continuous improvement framework.

4. Lack of a visible Mission Message (Example: "As a member of this Community, you're part of a family. As a family we are on a mission to prepare you to be independent, contribute to your community and live your life to the fullest. Your contribution is so valuable we cannot risk it. Let's work together, as a team, to prepare you for the task ahead by supporting your individuality, clearing a path for you to excel and connect you to it."). - As I walked around all of the schools, I could not help but notice the amount of empty wall space, especially in teacher and administrator group work spaces.

    A "Mission", in any organization, is a "living, breathing life form", directed by the superintendant and driven home by messages from staff. The customer (community, parents/guardians and students) provides feedback that helps determine the best direction.

5. Pride and PIE – The final and most impressive introduction that I witnessed was at the high school with "Pride" Teacher/Mentors. These mentors work with students one on one on a weekly basis using "Proactive Intervention Strategies" that allow students to progress independently and at peak levels. These interactions are not

curriculum based but more intervention, connection and enrichment focused. Mentors have access to many important tools such as tutoring and support, guidance counseling, social workers, health care providers, learning disability assessment and even community outreach programs. These mentors stay involved in the student's high school experience all four years to give the best chance for student success.

This program seems to be the best strategy for closing the gaps in the district's mission at all levels.

JUSTIFICATION

Instruction - Corporate Automated Differentiated Instruction Programs (CADIPs)

I have a copy of a Lesson Plan from "CNC Machining Technology" from the shop where I used to work.

This program was written in the shop by instructors for use by apprentices, new hires and machinists requiring refresher retraining.

Picture a classroom with twenty workstations, all networked together and connected to two CNC Vertical Mills and two CNC Lathes in the front of the classroom.

All students used the same interfaces for CAD (Computer Assisted Drafting), CAM (Computer Assisted Machining) and Simulators (3D Models with animation for simulating manufacturing processes on machine tools) just like what is used on the machine shop floor.

Students were given drawings of a bolt (to be manufactured on CNC Lathe) and a rectangular fixture (to be machined on the CNC Vertical Mill). Students had to draw the parts in the CAD package, assign code to machine the part in the CAM package and finally run a simulator to be sure the parts could be manufactured to specification.

Students could then download the program to the machines at the front of the classroom and manufacture the parts. If parts were found to be within tolerance, the instructor would sign off the parts to certify the student had satisfactorily completed the course.

What is unique about this class is that students moved independently through the material while instructors were moving up and down the aisles to give assistance where it was needed even though each student may be at a different stage in the course.

Because each student moved throughout the course at their own speed, the four machines at the front of the classroom were able to support the class of twenty students.

This lesson plan is from 1993…more than 25yrs ago.

This style of instruction challenges instructors to create an environment that lets students move through the material independently and at peak levels and allows teaching and learning to go from a "one size fits all" to "individual tutoring in a classroom environment".

AUDITING AND AUDIT MATERIALS

I. Auditing Documents
   a. Chapter 7 - Summary Outline
   b. Chapter 3 – School Committee and Superintendant
   c. Chapter 4 - Teaching
   d. Chapter 5 – General Structure (Checklist)
   e. Chapter 6 – Career Preparation Process
II. Research
   a. Local Educational Agency
      1) Vision
      2) Mission
      3) Time Line and Milestones
      4) Safety (Attendance)
      5) Quality Definition
      6) Beneficial Suggestion Program (_Electronic Application, _Database, _Statuses, _Cost Justification, _Procedure, _Timeline and Milestones, _Reviewable by the Community, _Estimated vs. Actual Value)
      7) Curriculum
         a/ Proficiency Based
            1- Proficiency Based Learning
               a) Break down Skills into manageable steps
               b) Understanding of Requirements
               c) Learning Gaps
               d) Proficient Performance of Requirements
            2- Staff Requirements
               a) Teachers held to minimum metric requirements
               b) Administrators insure Instructional Pedagogy
               c) Elected Officials maintain metric requirements

8) Lesson Plans and Programs
    a/ Academic Groups - Teacher Guided, Study Strategies (Structure, Skills, Time Management, Reps, priorities), Test Taking Skills(Structure, Skills, Time Management, guessing, priorities)
    b/ Corporate Level Differentiated Instruction Programs Procurement
        1- Evaluate with Metrics
        2- Guaranteed Improvement
        3- Company Setup and Train
        4- Software Customization

9) Students - Career Guidance

10) Staff - Evaluations, Prof Development, Job Descriptions, Recruiting

11) School Board Agendas and Minutes Review - 6mo.

12) Carryout Mission "A Living Being".
    a/ Core Subject Areas – Communication, Social Acceptance, Management, Special Needs, Standards Based Learning, Philosophy, Leadership, Inspirational Message
    b/ Staff Direction – Admin, Teachers, Volunteers etc.
        1- Total staff buy-in on where Department is going.
        2- Proactive Intervention for Assured Student Connectedness
        3- All staff part of the Mission
        4- Release of non-effective staff.
    c/ Celebrations of Achievement - Art, Music, STEM, SRTC, Academics, Athletics etc.
    d/ Family Orientation Days (Open House, First Days, Retreats)
        1- Future/Past Stories
        2- Team Building
        3- Soldier Reach-out
        4- Celebration of Achievement
    e/ Daily Inspiration to all Students – "We will never give up on you"
        1- Fill Walls - Teacher/Admin Spaces.
        2- Include in all discussions
        3- Constant and Logical Progression

13) Interviews – Former Parents, Students

14) District and School Website Reviews

EDITORIAL

AN INFORMATION SESSION ENTITLED "HIDDEN IN PLAIN SIGHT"

Back in May of 2019 an information session entitled "Hidden in Plain Sight" sponsored by the Police Department, The "Choose to be Healthy Coalition" and the school department was held for parents and members of the community.

In this presentation one room in the high school was setup to simulate a typical teenager's bedroom that contains devices used to conceal contraband. After hearing of this presentation a few thoughts came to mind.

First, contrary to popular opinion, students are not criminals. I am wondering if the police department, The Choose to be Healthy Coalition and the school department would be so receptive to this strategy if it meant that I would be coming to their home unannounced to do a search, maybe through their underwear drawer, to find anything that may be viewed as objectionable. I'm sure the police department would be the first to point out that you would "need a warrant for that".

Secondly, if during one of these searches parents did come across a hiding place containing contraband then they are already in the middle of a dire situation and the road back to trust between parents and students may be long and difficult.

As health care professionals love to tell us over and over, "substance use disorders" have three major areas of focus…prevention, treatment and recovery. Since treatment and recovery deal with the situation after the fact our focus needs to be on prevention.

This would come as a result of collaboration between educators, parents and the community. We need our students to know that as a member of this community, they're part of a family. As a family we are on a mission to prepare them to be independent, contribute to society and live their lives to the fullest. Their contribution is so valuable we cannot risk it. We need to work together, as a team, to prepare them for the task ahead by supporting their individuality, clearing a path for them to excel and connect them to it.

EDITORIAL

CORPORATE AUTOMATED DIFFERENTIATED INSTRUCTION PROGRAMS

My name is Edsel Shejen and I live in York, Maine. I was born and I grew up in York and went to York Schools. After Graduating, I attended a local trade school for Machine Tool Processes and spent thirty six years in manufacturing.

After I retired, I decided to take the problem solving skills that I had learned and apply them to education.

I have here a copy of a Lesson Plan for "CNC Machining Technology".

This program was written in the shop by instructors for use by apprentices, new hires and machinists requiring refresher retraining.

Picture a classroom with twenty workstations, all networked together and connected to two CNC Vertical Mills and two CNC Lathes in the front of the classroom.

All students used the same interfaces for CAD (Computer Assisted Drafting), CAM (Computer Assisted Machining) and Simulators (3D Models with animation for simulating manufacturing processes on machine tools) just like what is used on the machine shop floor.

Students were given drawings of a bolt (to be manufactured on CNC Lathe) and a rectangular fixture (to be machined on the CNC Vertical Mill). Students had to draw the parts in the CAD package, assign code to machine the part in the CAM package and finally run a simulator to be sure the parts could be manufactured to specification.

Students could then download the program to the machines at the front of the classroom and manufacture the parts. If parts were found to be within tolerance the instructor would sign off the parts to certify the student had satisfactorily completed the course.

What is unique about this class is that students moved independently through the material while instructors were moving up and down the aisles to give assistance where it was needed, even though each student may be at a different stage in the course.

Because each student moved throughout the course at their own speed, the four machines at the front of the classroom were able to support the class of twenty students.

If you look at this lesson plan you will see that it is from 1993.

This style of instruction challenges instructors to create an environment that lets students move through the material independently and at peak levels and allows teaching and learning to go from a "one size fits all" to "individual tutoring in a classroom environment".

EDITORIAL

EDUCATIONAL STRATEGY PK12
AUDIT SUMMARY SPEECH

My name is Edsel Shejen, I was born and grew up in York, Maine and went to York schools. After graduating, I attended a local trade school for Machine Tool Processes and spent thirty six years in manufacturing.

During that time, there were four metrics that were drilled into our heads - Safety, Quality, Schedule and Cost. We would say that we wanted to "safely, produce a quality product, on time at the lowest cost".

After these metrics were established, the departments within the shop used problem solving systems such as Lean Manufacturing, Deming Principles and Quality Circles to identify problems, determine causes and implement solutions that gave the greatest impact for the least cost. After implementation, we monitored metrics to determine the effectiveness of our recommendations.

After I retired from manufacturing I decided to take the problem solving skills that I had learned and apply them to education.

I organized these skills into the form of an audit and conducted that audit on the school district in my area.

The audit included:

1. A review of the district and school websites
2. Interviews with former students and parents.
3. Attending six months of school committee meetings and review of meeting minutes.
4. A Review of federal and state assessments of the schools in the district.

These were my recommended actions:

I. Develop a Team Oriented District Mission - Develop a mission oriented culture, determine goals as a metric definition of the mission and include requirements, timeline and milestones for funding, technical support and legal action.

II. Creation of a Strategic Plan to Complete the Mission - Adopt a proven, superior, education plan that is aligned with the district's mission, is based on continuous improvement principles, and includes an option to modify or drop it when not living up to expectations.

III. Communication to the Public through an Education Dashboard - Display for review by the community in an Education Dashboard "real time" metrics that measure successes and are a definition of the district's mission.

IV. Staff Development Strategies – The district will need to review the involvement, relationship and effectiveness of performance evaluations, professional development, position descriptions and personnel recruitment strategies within a continuous improvement framework as it relates to student peak performance.

V. Effective Corporate Automated Differentiated Instruction Programs (CADIPs) - Implement intuitive teaching programs that are based on individual tutoring in a classroom environment, where students can progress independently and at peak levels. (Kahn Academy, IXL)

VI. Proactive Intervention Strategy (Basic Needs, Behavior and Academic Guidance)

   a. Community Support Programs - Determining the extent of involvement in community support programs is a great way to start to determine the numbers of students committed to the mission, but after these basic numbers are established we need to go deeper. Prioritization of the remaining individual students at risk, will give a better idea of the work involved in completing the mission.

   b. "Teach/Learn" mode vs. "Infraction/Penalty" mode - Don't institute a penalty to avoid a learning moment. Wide sweeping policies that group students together to apply a single remedy for what may be a very individual and personal situation, only aggravates an already difficult situation. There are no shortcuts to keeping students on track. Every student requires connectivity to achieve peak performance.

   c. Academic Intervention Strategies - Using continuous improvement principles, utilize a tiered approach in dealing with struggling performance. Support systems, skill enhancement and specialized instruction may be needed, while not forgetting connectedness.

   d. Required Connectivity - Initiating interventions for wellbeing, behavior, special needs, motivation etc. and insuring engagement through STEAM, extra-curricular activities, nature based programs, entrepreneurship etc. is a more direct approach in helping students connect to the best path.

e. Career Development (Professional, Kinetic or Both) – This is the minimum required message to students going forward: "As a member of this Community, you're part of a family. As a family we are on a mission to prepare you to be independent, a contributor to your community and live your life to the fullest. Your contribution is so valuable we cannot risk it. Let's work together, as a team, to prepare you for the task ahead by supporting your individuality, clearing a path for you to excel and connect you to it."

f. Continuous Determination of Need – We will conduct a thorough search, using continuous improvement principles, for any potential student in our area of responsibility that has a need for assistance.

As for a current update, the good news is many of the issues outlined above have been addressed and after gathering metrics, we can review the effects of these actions on outcomes.

EDITORIAL

LIFE IS FRAGILE

My godson is a bagpiper, at 16 he played at a funeral for one of his classmates that was killed in a car accident. When the service was over friends and family, with tears in their eyes, thanked him for his contribution and well wishes, but the truth was, he didn't understand what had just happened either.

It is alarming to me the direction that future generations seem to be taking. We are so afraid as adults to tell them the realities of this life…"life is fragile".

As parents and members of the community we rightly take so much care in the preparation of our children for the future. The years of school, activities, pursuits of excellence and all the while never telling them the harsh reality that one look away from the road to your phone can take it all away in one instant, leaving parents, family, friends, teachers, coaches and classmates all suffering and wondering what went wrong. Yes, future generations have to know they hold some responsibility in these life changing split second decisions.

It's disturbing to me that the very people who want to teach this lesson to our children are fired from their jobs because parents and members of the community do not want to have their children exposed to these harsh realities.

No, not everyone is going to succeed, some will not make it. Not everyone is going to get that trophy at the end of the race. The best chance of getting that trophy is in choosing the best race to run and making the best preparations for it. Even then, they still may not win that race. One thing is for sure, giving up is not an option.

Future generations need to know that as members of their community, they're part of a family. As a family we are on a mission to prepare them to be independent, contribute to their' community and live their lives to the fullest. They need to know their contribution is so valuable we cannot risk it. We need to work together, as a team, to prepare them for the task ahead by supporting their individuality, clearing a path for them to excel and connecting them to it.

EDITORIAL

PERFORMANCE EVALUATIONS AND INSTITUTIONS OF HIGHER LEARNING

One added benefit from performance evaluations may be in helping to determine whether institutions of higher learning are producing effective teachers from day one.

A common theme whether it's in the media or from friends that are teachers is "When I first started teaching I didn't know how to teach."

Since these teachers may have spent in excess of two hundred thousand dollars on their degree, this is a bit alarming.

How did we arrive here? I have a couple of theories;

> First, it would seem that most institutions of higher learning view teaching as more of a theoretical endeavor than the development of a skill. Just dropping a student teacher into an internship atmosphere alongside an experienced teacher does not insure that graduates will be ready to manage a classroom on day one.

> Secondly, I believe most institutions of higher learning have forgotten what it is that they are there to do…turn students into teachers. Whether professors are spending their time providing philosophical insight on the latest education topic on PBS or submitting research opinions to legislative bodies, actually providing an education seems to have become of secondary importance.

In the shop we had apprentice instructors that machinists often went to for insight into the latest technology or manufacturing practice, but make no mistake, everyone knew what they were there to do…turn apprentices into machinists.

EDITORIAL

SERVICE

Service…How many really know the meaning of that word.

When our sons and daughters say they are "going into service" do they really understand what it means "to serve"? Do they want to give back to their community or do they just like the idea of "being in charge"?

Many of my family and friends, people I love, suffer with mental health and substance issues.

Multiple times I have been through that process of calling for help and end up watching these people I love being treated like criminals.

I've watched them be hand cuffed and strapped to a gurney for transport to the hospital.

I've watched them lay on a bed waiting to find out what comes next because nobody really knows.

I've seen doctors and nurses fighting over whether to continue medications because the original prescriber cannot be found.

I've watched as a stranger was assigned to their room to keep "watch" and I "watched" while this person knitted and stared into the eyes of this member of my family in an intimidating silence.

I've watched as the people I love were treated by their general practitioner like they had a broken leg because this "general practitioner" had no ability to deal with mental health issues and no mental health professionals were anywhere to be found.

I've been questioned by "Crisis Intervention Teams" that setup interviews with mental health professionals' days after the fact and the interviews took place in cold and impersonal video conferences because there was no one available to serve this function. Then, suddenly, the patient is stabilized and everything goes back the way it was.

Then it all starts all over again.

As a very close observer of these tragedies on multiple occasions, it is clear to me that mental health care is in need of a complete overhaul. Maybe an audit, by an independent firm is what is in order.

I hope this message may begin to spark some desperately needed dialog on this subject because right now…any start is a good start.

EDITORIAL

SUMMER SLIDE

While current metrics may show learning stagnation in area schools, they also reveal other issues such as chronic absenteeism and bullying.

Before we begin to look at things like "summer slide", going to school year round "like other countries" or other ways to increase the volume of work and thus cost, I hope we have done a thorough search for alternatives.

Developing a "Team Oriented District Mission Culture", inspired by positive messages, encouraging student individuality, connecting students to the best path, bringing people together through a common cause and success measured through the level of activity participation and future direction commitments.

Also I hope we have fully acknowledged the need for Corporate Automated Differentiated Instruction Programs (CADIPs). These programs focus on capabilities, capacity, continuity and efficacy providing a greater opportunity for analysis of instruction, especially when combined with performance evaluations and professional development.

EMAIL

BENEFICIAL SUGGESTION PROGRAMS

I would like to suggest the use of a beneficial suggestion program by area schools.

With so many ideas being thrown around for consideration, an organized way of assessing suggestions seems to be in order.

I have spent much time looking through the districts policies for any sign of a program like what we use in manufacturing but have not stumbled across anything.

If I have missed it then please disregard this email. If the district is in need of a formal system for handling expressed needs and justifications with estimated payback I have attached a policy used by the United States Office of Personnel and Management for setting up such a system.

With so many needs and limited funds an organized approach seems a good place to start.

Thanks for listening, once again, and this is "Education from a Manufacturing Perspective".

EMAIL

DEVELOPING UNITY

My name is Edsel Shejen and I was born and grew up in York, Maine and went to York Schools.

After Graduating, I attended a local trade school for Machine Tool Processes and spent thirty six years in manufacturing. After I retired, I decided to take the problem solving skills that I had learned and apply them to education.

I was glad to read about inclusion training for coaches in area schools and the formation of an Athletic Advisory Council. I'm hoping that this council will become an "Activities Advisory Council" at some later date.

I am also hoping this training demonstrated the advantages to unity and multiple views through examples of beneficial outcomes whether they are environmental, humanitarian or just monetary.

Finally I hope there will be the creation of a metric to measure activity participation as this would be a great way to begin to determine the level of commitment to the school's mission. The use of this data over time may determine future trends in connectivity.

REFERENCES

1   Elementary Secondary Education Act of 1965
2   No Child Left Behind Act of 2001
3   Every Student Succeeds Act of 2015
4   Website Scout.com
5   Website Maxpreps.com
6   Website Rivals.com
7   Website National Underclassmen Combine
8   Website National Collegiate Scouting Association
9   Website Petersons.com
10 Website nces.ed.gov/collegenavigator
11 Website federalstudentaid.ed.gov
12 Website noodle.org
13 Website scholarships.com
14 Website collegeanswer.com
15 Website collegetoolkit.com
16 Website collegenet.com
17 Website mesfoundation.com
18 Website collegeview.com
19 Website schoolsoup.com
20 Website studentaid.com
21 Website finaid.com
22 Website studentaid.ed.gov
23 Website students.gov
24 Website fafsa.com
25 Website profileonline.collegeboard.com
26 Website commonapp.com
27 Website netprocecalculator.collegeboard.com
28 Website fafsa4caster.ed.gov
29 Beyond Financial Aid Handbook
30 Family and Community Engagement Handbook
31 School Safety Report
32 Section504 Guidelines
33 USA Government Branches Report
34 NCTQ Criterion Referenced Teaching Degree Programs
35 NCTQ The Science of Learning
36 MeDHHS Reference Book 2010